THE OWL AND THE WOODPECKER

For Rebecca

THE OWL AND

London OXFORD UNIVERSITY PRESS 1971

THE WOODPECKER

Brian Wildsmith

Once upon a time,
in a forest, far away,
there lived
a Woodpecker.

The Woodpecker lived in
a tree in which he slept all
night and worked all day.

In the tree next door,
there came to live an
Owl, who liked to
work all night and sleep
all day.

The Woodpecker
worked so hard
and made so much
noise that his
tapping woke the
Owl.
"I say, you, there!"
screeched the
Owl. "How can I
possibly sleep
with all that
noise going on?"
"This is my tree,"
the Woodpecker
said, "and I shall
tap it as I please."

The Owl lost his temper. His screeches and hoots echoed through the forest, and animals for miles around came running to see what was the matter.

"You carry on tapping, Master Woodpecker,"
squeaked the mouse. "Owl is always bossing
and chasing us about."

"Oh, do be quiet," growled the Bear. "Woodpecker, stop tapping, and let Owl sleep. We
like a peaceful life around here."

Angrily, the Owl swooped down
on the small animals, who ran for
their lives and hid in all kinds of
curious places. "Bully," they
shouted, when they were sure
they were safe.

Then the Owl asked the bigger animals what he could do
to stop the noise, but they all shook their heads.
"How should we know?" they said. "You are the wise and
clever one. Perhaps you could move to another tree."

"Why should I?" snapped the Owl. "I like living in this tree. That noisy Woodpecker must move."

But the Woodpecker would not move. Day after day his noisy tapping kept the Owl awake. And day after day the Owl became more tired and more and more bad-tempered. He began to be so crotchety and rude that all the other animals decided that something must be done.

So they held a meeting.
"Something must be done," said the Badger.
"Woodpecker was here first, so Owl must leave."

"But he says he will not leave his tree," replied the Deer.
"In that case we shall have to push down the tree, and then
he will have to leave," said the crafty Fox.

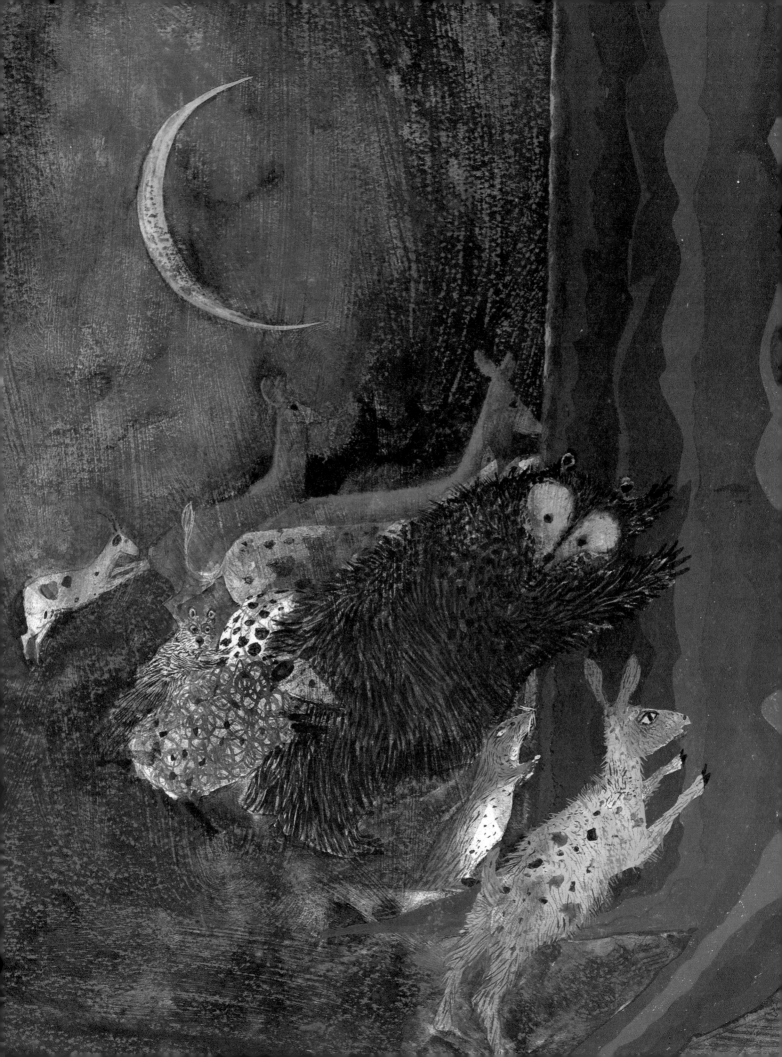

That night while the Owl was out hunting they all tried to push down his tree. But no matter how hard they pushed and puffed and panted they could not move the tree the smallest bit. So they gave up, and went back home.

Some time later two strangers came to the forest. They were a pair of beavers, and they took a fancy to the Owl's tree, and started to gnaw at the trunk.

Every day they gnawed a little more, until it seemed as if they would gnaw the trunk right through.

Then one day a great storm shook the forest. The wind roared through the trees. It was so strong the Woodpecker gave up tapping, and so for once the Owl slept in peace.

The Owl's tree began to creak and crack and groan as the wind grew more and more fierce, but the tired Owl slept soundly on.

Suddenly the Woodpecker saw the Owl's tree begin to

sway and fall. At once he struggled bravely through the
storm and tapped loudly close to the Owl's ear to wake
him. The Owl woke up in a fury, hearing the Woodpecker
tapping on his tree, but when he realized his tree was being
blown down his anger quickly disappeared. Together the
Woodpecker and the Owl struggled to safety just as the
tree crashed to the ground.

Then the storm died away, and the Owl thanked the Woodpecker for saving his life. Now he was glad that the Woodpecker had been his neighbour.

So the Owl and the Woodpecker became good friends,
and the Woodpecker helped the Owl to find another
tree in a quiet part of the forest, where he could sleep
all day without being disturbed.
Peace and quiet returned to the forest and the Owl and
the Woodpecker remained good friends all the rest of
their lives.

Oxford University Press, Ely House, London W.1 GLASGOW NEW YORK TORONTO MELBOURNE WELLINGTON CAPE TOWN IBADAN NAIROBI DAR ES SALAAM LUSAKA ADDIS ABABA
DELHI BOMBAY CALCUTTA MADRAS KARACHI LAHORE DACCA KUALA LUMPUR SINGAPORE HONG KONG TOKYO ISBN 0 19 279676 3 © Brian Wildsmith 1971. First published 1971.
Reprinted 1974. *All rights reserved. No part of this publication may be reproduced, stored in a retrieval system, or transmitted, in any form or by any means, electronic, mechanical,
photocopying, recording or otherwise, without the prior permission of Oxford University Press.* Printed in Austria.